This is the story of the three Wise Men
as told by St Matthew. The same story
was carved on four stone capitals
in the cathedral of Autun in Burgundy
by the great medieval sculptor Gislebertus

There are four scenes :
the Wise Men before Herod
the Adoration of the Wise Men
the Dream of the Wise Men
the Flight into Egypt

In their explanatory text
Régine Pernoud and Canon Grivot
discuss the work of Gislebertus
and the role of the cathedral
in the everyday life of the Middle Ages

THE STORY
OF THE
WISE
MEN

According to the Gospel of Saint Matthew

Holt, Rinehart and Winston, Inc. Publishers

New York · Chicago · San Francisco

with the Trianon Press · Paris

Now when Jesus was born in Bethlehem of Judea

in the days of Herod the king,

behold, wise men from the East came to Jerusalem, saying,

'Where is he who has been born king of the Jews?

For we have seen his star in the East,

and have come to worship him.'

When Herod the king heard this, he was troubled,

and all Jerusalem with him;

and assembling all the chief priests

and scribes of the people, he inquired of them

where the Christ was to be born.

They told him, 'In Bethlehem of Judea;

for so it is written by the prophet:

"And you, O Bethlehem, in the land of Judah,

are by no means least among the rulers of Judah;

for from you shall come a ruler

who will govern my people Israel." '

Then Herod summoned the wise men secretly

and ascertained from them what time the star appeared;

and he sent them to Bethlehem, saying,

'Go and search diligently for the child,

and when you have found him bring me word,

that I too may come and worship him.'

When they had heard the king they went their way;

and lo, the star which they had seen in the East

went before them, till it came to rest

over the place where the child was.

When they saw the star,

they rejoiced exceedingly with great joy;

and going into the house

they saw the child with Mary his mother,

and they fell down and worshiped him.

Then, opening their treasures,

they offered him gifts,

gold and frankincense and myrrh.

* * *

And being warned in a dream

not to return to Herod,

they departed to their own country by another way.

Now when they had departed,

behold, an angel of the Lord

appeared to Joseph in a dream and said,

'Rise, take the child and his mother,

and flee to Egypt,

and remain there till I tell you;

for Herod is about to search for the child,

to destroy him.'

And he rose and took the child

and his mother by night,

and departed to Egypt,

and remained there until the death of Herod.

This was to fulfil what the Lord

had spoken by the prophet,

'Out of Egypt have I called my son.'

Then Herod, when he saw that he had been tricked

by the wise men, was in a furious rage,

and he sent and killed all the male children

in Bethlehem and in all that region

who were two years old or under,

according to the time which he had ascertained

from the wise men. Then was fulfilled

what was spoken by the prophet Jeremiah:

'A voice was heard in Ramah, wailing and loud lamentation,

Rachel weeping for her children;

she refused to be consoled, because they were no more.'

But when Herod died,

behold, an angel of the Lord appeared in a dream

to Joseph in Egypt, saying,

'Rise, take the child and his mother,

and go to the land of Israel,

for those who sought the child's life are dead.'

And he rose and took the child and his mother,

and went to the land of Israel.

But when he heard that Archelaus

reigned over Judea in place of his father Herod,

he was afraid to go there,

and being warned in a dream

he withdrew to the district of Galilee.

And he went and dwelt in a city called Nazareth,

that what was spoken by the prophets might be fulfilled,

'He shall be called a Nazarene.'

★ ★ ★

GISLEBERTUS OF AUTUN

Notes on his work and the role of the Cathedral
in the everyday life of the Middle Ages
by Régine Pernoud and Canon Grivot

Gislebertus hoc fecit · Gislebertus made this

AUTUN is like many other small towns in that part of France which is still called Burgundy, even though the Duchy of Burgundy[1] long ago vanished from the map. It is tucked neatly into the side of a hill, its spires rising above the pleasant, rather undistinguished countryside that surrounds it. There are still several landmarks to indicate that once it was one of the largest cities of Roman Gaul (its name comes from the Latin *Augustodunum*,[2] town of Augustus Caesar), and that later in the Middle Ages it was one of the busiest and most important towns in Burgundy.

The streets of Autun, narrowing as they wind uphill, all lead to the cathedral, the heart and center of its medieval past. A large porch covers the steps going up to its entrance. Above the double door, framed in a triple arch, is a spectacle which was carved 800 years ago to greet every visitor to the cathedral, and still has the power to move us to wonder and awe. A towering figure of Christ in Majesty, seated on a throne with His arms outstretched, is presiding at the Day of Judgement. On Christ's right is Paradise where the Virgin Mary, with St Peter and the apostles, is waiting to welcome the elect. On His left lies the region of eternal damnation where those who have been judged and found wanting are seized by fearful-looking devils. Below, the souls of the dead are rising from their coffins and going to the reward their good or evil actions have earned them (pp. 30-31).

Every detail of this pageant in stone has been carved with compassion, often with humor. On Christ's right a child is getting a helping hand up to heaven from a friendly angel while St Peter, with an enormous key over his shoulder, is holding the upstretched hands of another soul (p. 39); on the left of Christ, at the 'weighing of the souls', St Michael's adversary is a huge devil who has put another smaller devil onto his side of the scales and is trying to tilt the balance in his favor; below Christ on the lintel,[3] an angel with drawn sword, who separates the damned from the elect, is turning

[26]

Angel separating the damned from the elect
(Detail of the lintel)
Above, the artist's signature

GISLEBERTVS HOC FECIT

back a particularly disappointed-looking suppliant (see the previous page).

When you examine this dramatic scene more closely, you will notice two sets of Latin inscriptions which underline the visual story—one around the mandorla[4] on which Christ is carved:

> *I alone dispose of all things and crown the just,*
> *Those who follow crime I judge and punish;*

the other on the band which separates the lintel from the tympanum[5] proper, the first part above the elect:

> *Thus shall rise again everyone who does not lead a sinful life,*
> *And endless light of day shall shine for him;*

and the second above the damned:

> *Here let fear strike those whom earthly error binds,*
> *For their fate is shown by the horror of these figures.*

In the center of this inscription there are three words which are quite out of keeping with the other texts: GISLEBERTUS HOC FECIT (Gislebertus made this). These words are the artist's signature and tell us the name of the creator of this masterpiece. It is a remarkable thing, this signature. Even today, when a work of art is almost always signed, it would be surprising to find an artist's signature so large and so conspicuously placed. Gislebertus's signature is at the very center of the Last Judgement scene, exactly below Christ, and is over two feet in length. In the 12th century, when the tympanum of Autun was carved, very few works were signed at all; anonymity was the general rule. Of the scores of architects, sculptors, painters, scribes and illuminators of manuscripts who worked in the Romanesque[6] period, we know hardly any by name. It cannot be simple chance that gave Gislebertus this place of honor. He must have been held in great esteem by the bishop and chapter[7] who commissioned the work, to have been allowed to sign his name in such a place of prominence.

About Gislebertus the man, apart from his name, we unfortunately know very little—nothing, in fact, of the events of his personal life. No written records refer to him; no folk memory of him survives. His signature on the tympanum remains the only clue to his identity. However, scholars and archaeologists are agreed that, besides the tympanum which he signed, Gislebertus was responsible for practically all the sculpture in the cathedral, including the four beautiful capitals[8] which in the preceding pages tell the story of the Wise Men and the childhood of Christ.

By comparing Gislebertus's sculpture at Autun with carvings found elsewhere, it has been possible to get some idea of his background. Before coming to Autun in about 1125, he was probably working at Vézelay,[9] for several fragments in his unmistakable style have been found there. It was at Vézelay that St Bernard[10] preached his historic sermon rallying the people to the cause of the Second Crusade. There is little doubt that Gislebertus's whole life was spent in Burgundy (his work is not found anywhere else in France), and as a young man he probably received his training as a sculptor at the famous abbey of Cluny.[11] This was the center of learning and the arts during that period, and the abbey church was the largest building in Christendom (larger even than St Peter's at Rome). It is unbelievable that the walls of this great church were torn down at the time of Napoleon and its stones later sold to building contractors in near-by Lyon. We do not know what happened to our artist after he completed the tympanum at Autun, probably about 1140. For there is no further trace of any sculpture by him either at Autun or elsewhere.

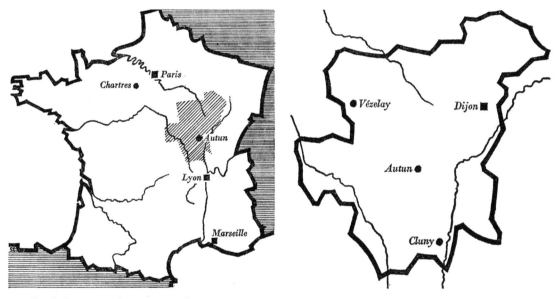

Gislebertus has now been restored to his rightful place as perhaps the greatest sculptor of medieval Europe, but for centuries both the artist and his work were forgotten. In fact, the great tympanum that he signed was actually covered with plaster for a long period during the 18th and 19th centuries. Only in recent times were the first sculptures by him at Autun 're-discovered'. They had been hidden behind the marble facing which was added to the apse[12] of the church in the 18th century and was only removed a few months before the war in 1939. Finally the head of the majestic Christ of the Last Judgement was found by chance among some abandoned sculpture in the museum of Autun and was put back in its rightful place in 1948.

Among the earliest sculptures that Gislebertus carved at Autun are the four capitals which tell the story of the Wise Men. In the 19th century, the pillars in the choir[13] on which these capitals stood had to be repaired. The

[29]

capitals were taken down and were damaged in the process, the 'Wise Men before Herod' particularly badly; but it is some compensation that we can see them today in the cathedral museum at eye-level.

What a lot of love and careful detail Gislebertus lavished on these small figures (on a very different scale from the monumental tympanum he was to sign), as he illustrated St Matthew's story verse by verse. There are the Wise Men, the three kings from the east, dismounted from their horses after their journey and listening carefully to Herod before they set out to find the king of the Jews. Then, guided by the star, they reach their destination and present their gifts: the Child Jesus, much intrigued, is trying to open the casket He is offered, while one of the Wise Men, lost in wonder, gravely takes off his crown. Round the corner of this capital, out of sight and a little out of things, sits Joseph pensively, with his chin in his hand.

The next scene is the Dream of the Wise Men. They are lying side by side under a handsomely embroidered cover (of course they have their crowns on—how else would you know a king in bed?). A dream is a difficult thing to illustrate. Gislebertus solved the problem by carving an angel, the messenger of God, as he is delivering His warning: the angel points to the star which will guide the Wise Men home, and wakes one of them, while the other two are still fast asleep.

Then it is Joseph's turn to be warned of the danger threatening Christ. He has saddled his donkey, seated Mary and the Child on its back, and set off on the Flight into Egypt. The orb, symbol of Christ's dominion over the world, is too heavy for a small boy, so His Mother carries it for Him; He rests one hand on it as a king should, and with the other holds fast to her arm for safety. Joseph scans the road ahead with anxious eyes, pulling on the halter, while the donkey picks his feet up briskly as if well aware of his important mission. Did Gislebertus carve him from life, or from some 12th-century ancestor of the wooden donkey on wheels that was still led through the churches in Alsace on Palm Sunday, not so long ago?

It is impossible, in fact, to separate the sculptures that decorate Romanesque capitals from the life that went on around them or the atmosphere in which they were conceived. If Gislebertus followed St Matthew's account as closely as he did, it was because he had been brought up on the Gospels; and the people who first admired his works could read the story in them as if St Matthew himself were speaking.

At that time the cathedral was not only a place of worship: it was a center of human activity where people gathered together, to pray, of course, but also to learn and even to be entertained. It was here that they came to be taught the Bible stories and the lives of the saints—for few people in those days could read or write—and to sing the psalms. All the figures carved on the capitals of a medieval church, or painted on its walls, are illustrations

[32]

Autun cathedral in the Middle Ages
(From an old painting)

of a world which was then as familiar to the ordinary man as his own: a world peopled by the apostles of the New Testament and the prophets of the Old, the kings and judges of Israel, and the saints of Christendom.

On high days and holy days the entire population assembled in the cathedral under the leadership of their bishop. They came from town and country alike, because the cathedral belonged not just to the city but to the whole diocese. This explains its great size. At Easter, Whitsun and Christmas, the people would flock there, vying with one another for the best places from which to follow the service, packed together in crowds denser than anything we can imagine today. The congregations were so large that it was out of the question to provide them with chairs or benches. Anyone who feared fatigue brought his own stool or sat on his folded coat. It was even necessary to organize one-way traffic, using the side aisles that run right and left of the nave[14] for this purpose. At the main entrance, with its three door-ways, one of the side doors would be used as an entry and the other as an exit; while the great center doorway was reserved for ceremonial processions of clergy and faithful, such as the procession on Palm Sunday when everyone carried a branch in memory of Christ's entry into Jerusalem.

On major feast-days, the liturgy often gave rise to a real theatrical performance, with the principal episodes being enacted by members of the clergy. At Easter, for instance, clerics dressed in white would take the part of the three holy women finding the tomb empty, and another, seated before the high altar, would be the angel greeting them in the words of the Gospel. Gislebertus's lovely capital showing the risen Christ with Mary Magdalen at His feet (p. 37) has this scene of the holy women and the angel carved on one side.

From simple acting out of the Bible story came more complicated plays. The oldest of these to be written in French (liturgical plays in Latin are mentioned as early as the 9th century) tells the story of the Creation, with Adam and Eve in the garden of Eden. Eve lets herself be tempted by the devil, who wins her with blandishments:

> *You are a weakly tender thing*
> *A rose is not so sweet...*

She falls a victim to his wiles and picks the forbidden fruit.

The carved figure of Eve actually exists at Autun. 'The most feminine figure of the Romanesque Middle Ages', a great art historian once called her. Beautiful, hesitant, looking back over her shoulder with an expression which is half-frightened, half-sly, she hides beneath the foliage of the Tree of Temptation and stretches out her hand for the apple. Eighty years ago this masterpiece was unknown. She is part of a lintel carved by Gislebertus for the north doorway of the church, which was taken down in the 18th century

[34]

Eve picking the apple
(Lintel of the old north doorway)

when Romanesque sculpture was out of fashion. The stones were destroyed or used in the construction of other buildings at Autun, and all trace of them was lost. It was only when a house was demolished at the end of the last century that Eve was found in its walls, miraculously almost intact. In her rightful place above the north doorway she would have been whispering in Adam's ear: we know from an early manuscript that his figure was carved on the other half of the lintel. Perhaps Adam, too, was used as a humble piece of masonry somewhere in Autun and one day a chance discovery will rescue him, as it did Eve, from oblivion.

Often these church plays would turn to comedy, for people at the time saw nothing irreverent in humor. So on Christmas night the congregation would wait with glee for Balaam and his ass to put in an appearance. The animal was a real figure of pantomime, played by two men under a piece of grey cloth; it indulged in all sorts of antics, braying and galloping about among the congregation, and wagging the ass's head that was part of its costume... Spectacles of this kind were not uncommon. There was even a special feast in the calendar to recall the ass's different roles in the Bible—the Flight into Egypt, for instance, or Christ's entry into Jerusalem. A live donkey was brought into church to mark the occasion, and when the clergy sang their verses, the people would respond with 'Hee-haw, hee-haw'!

There was also the feast of the Holy Innocents, the children whom Herod had massacred in his attempt to destroy the Infant Christ. It fell three days after Christmas and in its honor children were given the freedom of the church. One child dressed up as a bishop would sit on the bishop's throne; others took the canons' places in the stalls, and all of them were allowed to do exactly as they pleased. It was a wonderful opportunity to make fun of the clergy who were their teachers, to ridicule those they disliked, and generally to indulge in all the face-pulling and outrageous behavior they wanted—to such a point, in fact, that towards the end of the Middle Ages these holidays had got out of hand and had become so scandalous that they had to be stopped.

But in the 12th century the spirit was different, and no one thought anything of mixing fun with morality. Learned and ignorant, rich and poor, sick and well, all felt at home in the church. Even lepers, who were forced to live outside the town for fear of contagion, were able to visit Autun cathedral. This was because Autun was dedicated to their patron saint, St Lazarus (the brother of Martha and Mary Magdalen, whom Christ had raised from the dead),[15] and housed what were believed to be his relics.

It has been said that the large porch leading to the main entrance of the cathedral was reserved for the lepers, but in fact similar porches were built on to most of the pilgrimage churches. Vézelay, for instance, has a particularly fine one, completely covered in. The porches served as shelters for the pil-

[36]

Christ appearing to St Mary Magdalen
after His Resurrection
(Detail of capital)

grims or simply for the overflow from the church when it became too crowded. It was here too that alms were given to the poor and food to needy pilgrims, many of whom would be on their way to other shrines, Compostela perhaps, the shrine of St James the Apostle in Spain, whose pilgrims wore a cockle-shell as their distinctive badge. Gislebertus carved a Compostela pilgrim among the elect on the lintel at Autun, and next to him a man wearing a small cross on his pilgrim's scrip or pouch, to show he had made the even longer and more dangerous journey to the Holy Land. It was a great age for pilgrimages and a sacred duty to help all pilgrims on their way. In some years at Autun the cathedral distributed food to 18,000 people in a single day.

Autun's special feast was the first of September, the feast of St Lazarus. And on the same day as pilgrims flocked from far and near to do honor to the saint and ask his intercession, the citizens of Autun held their annual cattle-fair in the town. It would not have been uncommon to see a couple of traders shaking hands in the cathedral over a deal they had negotiated on the fair grounds, where hundreds of animals were lined up waiting to be led away by their new owners.

It was on cattle such as these—the great white oxen of the Charolais country whose descendants still breed prime beef for the French market—that the construction of the cathedral itself had depended. For twenty years and more long lines of them must have wound their way up the steep slope that led to the building site, slowly but surely pulling behind them huge blocks of stone hewn from the quarries. One after the other, the teams would work without a pause, laden now with the hard sandstone used for the foundations and bearing walls, and now with the beautiful limestone of Burgundy, soft enough for the sculptor's chisel but resistant to time and weather.

It was in this way that the great cathedrals, the 'white robe of churches' spoken of by a chronicler, came into being all over France. The entire resources of the country—its stone, its beasts of burden, the wood from its forests, the clay from its fields—all were pressed into service by men whose skill and sure artistic sense astonish us today: men like Gislebertus, in whose person we can pay tribute to the army of nameless builders who created Romanesque France, working in the face of odds that we, in an age of mechanization and rapid transport, find it hard to imagine.

If Gislebertus's name carved in fine letters on the tympanum is all that remains of the artist's identity, his sculptures are as alive today as they were 800 years ago. However fine its sculpture no other cathedral in France, even Chartres, has Autun's unity of style. From end to end of the cathedral Gislebertus illustrated the struggle between good and evil, the spiritual story of man from his fall with Adam and Eve to his redemption by Christ: Christ as the Child on His Mother's knee to His enthronement as the

[38]

St Peter with the key of heaven, and the apostles
(Detail of the tympanum)

Judge of all things. Gislebertus's work reflects not only the faith that inspired it. It brings back, too, the people for whom he interpreted the scriptures: the lord in his buckled cloak, the lady in her wide-sleeved dress, the working man, like Joseph, in his tunic and cap. In his carving of the resurrection of the dead on the lintel, the society which he knew comes to life: the bishop and abbot, with crozier and flowing robes; the monk in his rough woollen habit; the family—father, mother and child; the pilgrims, pack on shoulder, climbing to heaven as they had tramped the medieval roads; the children, and the humble believers; the sinner and wrongdoer, too.

In the medallions around the tympanum Gislebertus pictured the signs of the zodiac, man's temporal system, and the labors of the months, to show his familiar life of toil on the land: pruning the vines (this is Burgundy, one of the great vineyards of France), feeding the animals, threshing the grain, crushing the grape harvest for wine. For it was man whole and entire, his bodily existence as well as his soul, that was summoned to take part in the impressive scenes of the Second Coming.

Medieval man, as he entered Autun cathedral and looked up at Gislebertus's masterpiece over his head, could recognize himself in it and his whole world. It was on him that heaven was calling, for him the trumpets were sounding, in his favor that the scales were ready to turn, in his defence that St Michael was standing guard. The greedy, the proud and the vicious had fallen into the hands of the devil; but he could see the joy of the souls who had found their way to heaven. There was the Virgin Mary ready to welcome him. There was St Peter, keeper of the keys of heaven, with the other apostles. There, above all, surrounded by the sun, moon and stars, was Christ, Lord of the universe, with His arms open in invitation to all mankind to share His glory.

Christ in Majesty—'*I alone dispose of all things*'
(Detail of the tympanum)

Selected Glossary

[1] BURGUNDY did not become part of the French kingdom until 1477. In the Middle Ages it was a powerful and independent state (the Burgundians fought with the English against the French in the 100 Years' War), ruled by the Dukes of Burgundy, whose capital city was Dijon. It was the reigning Duke, Hugh II, who gave the land on which Autun cathedral was built. Today four *départements* or counties have taken Burgundy's place, one being *Saône-et-Loire* where Autun is situated.

[2] ROMAN AUTUN: *Augustodunum*, founded about 12 B.C., was built on an impressive scale, and became a celebrated center of culture and learning. Two of its main gateways are still standing.

[3] LINTEL: a block of stone (timber, etc.) placed horizontally over a door or other opening to carry the weight of the structure above. Medieval sculptors used this part of the framework in their designs. The Autun lintel shows the resurrection of the dead at the Last Judgement. Gislebertus carved another lintel at Autun (for the smaller north door, now demolished) with the figures of Adam and Eve to show the fall of man (p. 35).

[4] MANDORLA: an almond-shaped halo surrounding the full-length figure of Christ (the Virgin, etc).

[5] TYMPANUM: the surface area which is enclosed by a lintel below and an arch above. The medieval church-builders used this area for sculptures that would teach and inspire the people, while giving added splendor to the church entrance. The Autun tympanum is not only a beautiful work of art, it is also a masterpiece of construction. Huge in size, its base is about 7 yards wide, while the figure of Christ rises almost 10 feet high. It is carved over 29 different pieces of stone: easier for the sculptor to handle than a few large blocks but much harder to fit together afterwards.

[6] ROMANESQUE: the style of art and architecture in western Europe in the 11th and 12th centuries before the rise of Gothic. (In England the style is known as 'Norman', after the invaders who brought their own brand of Romanesque from the mainland.) The architecture in Burgundy was directly influenced by the remains of Roman civilization; and the sculpture is particularly fine.

[7] CHAPTER: the canons and clergy attached to a cathedral church and responsible under the bishop for its administration.

[8] CAPITAL: the stone at the top of a pillar or pilaster which bears the weight of the structure above. At Autun the interior capitals rest on flat, fluted pilasters (these were inspired by one of the Roman gateways in the town) and support the arches and ribs of the vaulted roof (see the view at the front of the book). About 50 of them are carved with scenes from the Bible and other sacred subjects. These alternate with foliage capitals, which are purely decorative.

[9] VÉZELAY, about 50 miles north-west of Autun, was a Benedictine abbey and a famous center of pilgrimage dedicated to St Mary Magdalen. Begun in 1096, the church is one of the most beautifully situated in France. It has a magnificent tympanum and many lovely sculptures; though its decoration was done by several different men and lacks the perfection and harmony of Autun.

[10] ST BERNARD (1091-1153), founder and abbot of the Cistercian monastery of Clairvaux, was one of the greatest figures of the Middle Ages, and a Burgundian by birth. On Easter Day 1146 he preached at Vézelay to the assembled lords of France, and fired them with such enthusiasm for the Second Crusade that he had to divide his own white habit among them so that they could sew Crusaders' crosses on their tunics there and then.

[11] CLUNY, about 40 miles south of Autun, was the greatest abbey of medieval France, founded by Benedictines early in the 10th century. Its influence spread throughout Europe, and at one time 1,450 other monasteries were under its control. Three successive churches were built at Cluny, the last and most splendid between 1088 and 1130. With an overall length of more than 200 yards, this was the largest building in Europe until St Peter's of Rome was rebuilt at the end of the 15th century. At the French Revolution, when monastic life and medieval architecture were both despised, the abbey was seized by the state and later sold for building material. The church was blown up in 1812 to make its demoli-

tion easier; and today all that remains are the south transept and tower, parts of the monastic buildings, and some capitals and other fragments.

12 APSE: the eastern end of the church which projects in a semi-circle behind the high altar.

13 CHOIR: the part of the church at the eastern end, below the high altar and above the nave, which was reserved for the clergy. They sang the services and were thus the 'choir'. Their wooden stalls can still be seen in many churches today.

14 NAVE: the main body of the church from the west door to the choir, usually divided from the aisles on either side by a row of pillars.

15 ST LAZARUS seems to have become the patron saint of lepers by association with the other Lazarus in the Gospel, the poor man of the parable who begged unsuccessfully at the rich man's gate and was covered with sores (*Luke*, xvi, 19-25).

The Plates

The plates in this book are from photographs by Franceschi and Ben Herb, and are taken from Gislebertus, Sculptor of Autun, *the definitive study by George Zarnecki and Denis Grivot, by courtesy of the publishers: in the U. S., the Orion Press, New York; in the U. K., the Trianon Press with Collins, London. The volume has been designed by Arnold Fawcus and produced by the Trianon Press, Château de Boissia, Clairvaux, Jura, France.*